Laugh O'Clock

Joke Book

For
Kids And Family

-HALLOWEEN EDITION-

With Fun
Illustrations

RIDDLELAND

Design elements from Freepik.com

Previously published as The Laugh Challenge Joke Book- Trick or Treat Edition by Riddleland

Table of Contents

Riddleland Bonus Book

http://pixelfy.me/riddlelandbonus

Thank you for buying this book. We would like to share a special bonus as a token of appreciation. It is a collection of 50 original jokes, riddles, and two super funny stories!

Join our **Facebook Group**
at **Riddleland for Kids** to get
daily jokes and riddles.

Introduction

"There is a child in every one of us who is still a trick-or-treater looking for a brightly-lit front porch."
— Robert Brault

Get ready to laugh! *It's Laugh O'Clock Joke Book: Halloween Edition* book is different from other joke books. This book is not meant to be read alone - although it can be; instead it is a game to be played with siblings, friends, family or between two people to see who can make the other laugh first. It's time to laugh; it's always laugh o'clock somewhere.

These jokes are written to provide a fun, quality reading experience. Children learn best when they are playing; reading is fun when it is something one wants to read, and most children want to read jokes. Reading jokes will increase vocabulary and comprehension. Jokes also have many other benefits:

• **Bonding** – Sharing this book is an excellent way for parents and children to spend some quality time having fun, sharing laughs, and making memories.

• **Building Confidence** - When parents ask one of the jokes, it creates a safe environment for children to burst out answers even if they are incorrect.
This helps the children to develop self-confidence and self-expression.

- **Improve Vocabulary** – Jokes are a lot of fun, and that makes reading a lot of fun. Children will need to understand the words if they want to understand the jokes.

- **Enhancing Reading Comprehension** – Many children can read at a young age but may not understand the context of words in the sentences. Jokes, especially puns, can help develop children's interest to comprehend the context.

- **Developing Creativity** – Funny, creative jokes can help children develop their sense of humor while getting their brains working. Many times a word in a joke can be taken two ways, and picturing it both ways leads to creative imagery.

- **Developing Logical Thinking Skills** – Because many jokes have a dual play on words, children must use logic to decide which meaning the speaker intended.

Enjoy the book, and, remember, it's always laugh o'clock somewhere.

Here are the rules!

The goal is to make your opponent laugh

- Face your opponent.

- Stare at them!

- Make funny faces and noises to throw your opponent off

- Take turns reading the jokes out loud to each other

- When someone laughs, the other person wins a point

First person to get 5 points, is crowned The Champion!

FUN FACTS FOR HALLOWEEN

Did you know that Jack-O'Lanterns have an Irish origin?

In folklore an Irishman called Stingy Jack tricked the devil and wasn't allowed to go to heaven or hell. He roamed the earth carrying a lantern, and people called him 'Jack of the Lantern' – it was thought that he tried to lure people off their paths, with the light from his lantern.

Do you know what the word 'witch' means?

The Old English meaning of wicce, means 'wise woman' and wiccan people were highly respected for their wisdom.

CHAPTER BONE
Question & Answer

"Pixie, kobold, elf and sprite, all are on their rounds tonight. In the wan moon's silver ray, thrives their helterskelter play." ~ **Joel Benton**

With the chapters named Bone, Boo, Thrill, and Gore instead of One, Two, Three, and Four, you can probably tell this book is going to be funny jokes about Halloween. The first chapter is called Bone for a reason - the bones are the skeleton, the foundation upon which the muscles hang; likewise, the questions answered here are the foundation for the rest of the book. Let's get right to them.

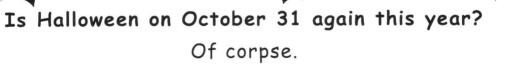

Is Halloween on October 31 again this year?

Of corpse.

What do you call somebody who is relaxed and not afraid on Halloween?

Scare-free, without a scare in the world.

What kind of lotion do ghosts put on themselves when they go to the beach?

Sun scream.

What do guy ghosts say to girl ghosts?

"Hello, boo-tiful."

What did Mom ghost instruct Junior ghost about his manners?

"Remember, don't spook until spooken to."

What military unit protects ghosts who haunt lighthouses?

The Ghost Guard.

Where do ghosts buy food?

At the ghost-ery store

Why did Mom scold Junior at the Halloween costume store when Junior asked for vampire teeth?

Because it's not polite to pick your teeth in public.

What are trick-or-treat agreements in which the child promises not to trick the adult if the adult will surrender a treat?

Trick-or-treaties.

What did the bird say on Halloween night when it rang doorbells?

"Trick or tweet."

Why do lights go out in thunderstorms?

Lights go on dates in all kinds of weather.

Where was Dad when the lights went out?

In the dark.

What does the tooth fairy call her Death costume?

The Grin Reaper.

After the journalist questioned the werewolf, who else did he want to talk to?

The who, what, when, why, and how wolves.

On what type of street do ghosts prefer to build their haunted houses?

Dead ends.

What kind of car do demons like to drive?

A coup devil.

Why are ghosts terrible liars?

You can see right through them.

What kind of ghosts have the best hearing?

The ear-iest.

What did the ghost of the rooster say?

"Cock-a-doodle-boo!"

How do ghosts prefer to show horror movies on their television?

On boo ray.

Where can missing ghosts be found?

At their favorite haunts.

What did the skeleton comedian identify as his funny bone?

The humorus.

Why didn't the skeleton propose to his girlfriend?

He didn't have the guts.

What did the trick-or-treaters nickname the pumpkin that called insults to everyone?

Jerk o' lantern.

Why is this a great joke book?

It has the Halloween spirit inside it.

What food items do ghosts frequently buy at the ghostery store?

Boo-berries, boo-ble gum, boo-loney, boo-rritos, blooderscotch syrup, cookies-and-scream I-scream, Dreaded Wheat cereal, French frights, ghoul ash, ham-boo-gers, grave-y, Rice Creepy cereal, spook-ghetti, and other ghost-eries.

What does Mom skeleton say to Junior skeleton each morning when she opens his curtains?

"Wake up, lazy bones."

Why didn't the skeleton eat any of the trick-or-treat candy?

He didn't have the stomach for it.

Why did the skeleton make poor decisions?

He was a bonehead.

What kind of lanterns do skeletons sometimes carry when they hunt the living?

Jack o' lanterns.

Why does the skeleton spend so much time reading?

He's trying to bone up.

Why wasn't the baby pumpkin allowed into the swimming pool?

There was no life gourd on duty.

Why was the jack-o-lantern depressed?

He was feeling a little empty inside.

Why should you never throw a ghost's boomerang?

It may come back to haunt you.

When do ghosts build snowmen?

In the dead of winter.

What kind of songs do ghosts like the most?

Haunting melodies.

Why did the jack o' lantern enjoy meditation?

He believed in inner light.

What did the ghosts say to each other on New Year's Eve?

"Happy Boo Year."

Did you hear the latest boos?

It's like a breath of fresh scare.

Why was the prince-turned-in-to-a-frog so worried about dying?

The wicked witch said he would croak.

What can you say in defense when your mom asks you if you are taking your brother's Halloween candy?

"Not really. I'm just helping him share."

Have you ever though about sneaking up on your alarm clock and yelling, "Boo!"?

Maybe then it will understand how you feel.

What kind of music do princes-turned-in-to-frogs prefer to listen to at the pond?

Hip hop.

What time is it when ghosts, werewolves, zombies, spiders, witches, warlocks, wizards, and/or skeletons begin to chase you?

Time to run!

When asked how he was doing, what did the pumpkin say?

"I'm vine; how are you doing?"

Why are jack-o-lanterns so forgetful?

They are empty headed.

17

What kind of milk product do farmers get from the nervous cows that graze near the haunted house?

Milk shakes.

What did one wall of the talking haunted house say to the other wall?

"I'll meet you at the corner."

After the witch turned the prince into a frog, he wrote a love letter to the princess. When he gave the letter to her, what did he say to her?

"Read it! Read it! Read it!"

What do you call a wicked witch thumbing for a ride at the side of the road?

A witch-hiker.

What do you call Death when he carries a broom instead of a scythe?

The Grim Sweeper.

How are a candle and a warlock alike?

They are both wicked.

How are a broom and a comb different?

Although both neaten things, witches can't ride on combs.

What happened when the girl enthusiastically bobbed for an apple?

She really sunk her teeth into it.

What two types of music do mummies prefer?

Ragtime and wrap.

What did the other scary creatures say on New Year's Eve?

"Happy New Fear."

Why did the jack o' lantern go to the hospital after Halloween?

He felt rotten.

Why did the mad scientist make cookies?

He thought he was making kookys.

Why wasn't the Invisible Man counted present at the mad scientist's party?

No one saw him.

If you were a mad scientist and melted crayons, candles, and perfumes into a living monster, what should you call the monster?

Frankincense.

When Dr. Frankenstein and his monster go trick-or-treating, what is it called when people give them a candy treat instead of letting them do a trick?

The bribe of Frankenstein.

What did the uncaring owl NOT do on Halloween?

Give a hoot.

What happened when the witch developed road rage?

She flew off the handle.

What does a pirate wear over his bad eye on Halloween?

A pumpkin patch.

What do witches use for a garage?

The broom-closet.

Are you friends with Mr. Jack O' Lantern?

If so, don't let people tell you that you don't know Jack.

Why did the schoolteacher like having jack o' lanterns as students?

She could tell when a light came on in their heads.

What has got to happen if my pumpkin is going to take first place in the jack-o-lantern contest?

I must make the cut.

What is the mad scientist's favorite type of dog?

A Lab.

Who works weekends at the haunted house scaring people?

Skeleton staff.

Are ghosts lonely?

They must be since they call everyone "boo".

Are ghosts committed to doing well?

They put the "dead" in dedicated.

What do you call a warlock's cat that has amassed a fortune?

A fat cat.

What charmed piece of clothing did the witch give to the baseball player to wear under his uniform?

Pantyhose: the pantyhose had runs.

How can you jinx a witch before she jinxes you?

Before she speaks, pu your arm in the air to give her a "high five"; she will become a victi of your "high" jinx.

What do warlocks rea the first thing every day to see what the day is going to be like?

Their horror-scope.

What's the problem with telling jokes about ghosts?

They have no substance.

How many warlocks does it take to change a lightbulb?

Only one; he'll change it into a frog.

How do monsters greet each other?

"Horror you doing?"

23

How did the skeleton know it was going to drizzle on Halloween?

He could feel it in his bones . . . plus he had heard the weather forecaster on the news the previous night.

What game does a baby ghost like to play with adult ghosts?

Peek-a-Boo-o-o-o-o-o-o.

How do ghosts build a haunted house?

They use boo prints.

How are sailors and warlocks alike?

Both are known for cursing.

Which ghost speaks o behalf of the other ghosts?

The spookesperson.

If a warlock turns a prince into a toad anc you come upon the toad, what should you say to it?

"Wart's happening?"

Which branch of the police arrested the black cat for destroying the warlock's curtains?

Claw Enforcement.

What do ghosts say to each other in passing?

"How do you boo?"

What did the warlock say to turn the friendly garden snake into a deadly poisonous snake?

"Abbra-ca-dabra, abbra-ca-cobra."

How do scary monsters like their steaks prepared?

Raw-w-w-w-w-w-w-w-w-w-w-w-w-w-w-w-w!

What will some monsters do if they get really, really mad?

Bite your head off – or at least try to.

How do you measure how fast a monster rips up flesh?

Mauls-per-hour.

How can you tell the age of a monster?

Count the number of rings under its eyes.

What can you find around the monsters' table?

Napkins, knives, forks, and goons.

Why did the monster take his trophy to the cemetery and toss it into an empty gravesite?

He wanted his trophy in-graved.

What did the monsters do after they successfully scared the children?

Gave each other a high nine.

What nickname was given to the zombie who could run a mile in a minute?

The zoom-bie.

Man's best friend is the dog, what is the werewolf?

Man's beast friend.

Is the moon evil?

Well, it does have a dark side.

How does a full moon stay in place?

Moonbeams.

How do girls usually fall in love with monsters?

It is love at first fright.

What do you call people who, on a full moonlit night, turn into storage facilities?

Werehouses.

How do monsters like their fried chicken?

"Terror-fried."

What kind of vehicle does a monster drive?

A monster truck.

What's the problem with being friends with Dracula?

He will suck the life out of you.

Where does Dracula like to stay on vacation?

A Bled and Breakfast.

Why do werewolves scratch themselves?

Because they know where it itches.

What do you tell Dracula after pranking him?

"I got you good, sucker."

What kind of ticks live on werewolves?

Lunar-ticks.

Where do ghosts like to go on summer vacation?

Lake Eerie.

What is the teenage werewolf's favorite hobby?

Collecting fleas.

What kind of ghost rides freight trains?

A hoboo.

How are readers of joke books and werewolves alike?

They both howl all night.

How do I know my girlfriend is a ghost?

I saw her come through a door.

What did Dracula dress in for the first day of the school year?

His bat-to-school clothes.

What happens when a baby ghost gets hurt playing Peeka-Boo-o-o-o-o-o-o?

She gets rushed to the I.C.U.

How angry can the werewolf get?

Howling mad.

Who appears on the front of *Ghosts Weekly* magazine?

The cover ghoul.

What's the difference between a werewolf and a flea?

One howls on the prairie and the other prowls on the hairy.

What happens to the werewolf every flea-dip day?

He becomes a wash-and-wear-wolf.

What is the name of the game that ghosts play where they hide and then try to scare each other?

Hide and Shriek.

What happened when the miser did not pay the priest for removing evil spirits from the furniture removed from the haunted house?

The furniture was repossessed.

What did the werewolf do with his Halloween candy?

He wolfed it down.

Why do ghosts tend to work as a team?

Because teamwork makes the scream work.

What did the werewolf say when asked how he was doing?

"I am a howling success; howl's it going with you?"

How does a ghost have a good time?

It lives a little bit.

Why is Dracula so against vegetarians?

He knows lots of vampires who have died from a wooden steak.

Even scary creatures have fears; what are Dracula's biggest fears?

Light, wooden stakes, and tooth decay.

What does Dracula like to do with his car?

Go on a blood drive.

What does Dracula stand on after soaking in the tub?

A bat mat.

What kind of car does Dracula drive?

A blood vessel.

Skeletons like all types of danger, but what is their very favorite type?

Grave danger.

Why did Dracula go to the blood bank?

He wanted to make a withdrawal.

What do you call a wolf that works as a guide dog for the blind?

A where wolf.

What was the lazy wizard known for casting instead of spells?

Fishing poles.

Why should you not grab a werewolf by its tail?

The end of the werewolf could be the end of you.

Why did the rotting zombie get to play quarterback on the football team?

Nobody does a handoff like he does it!

Where are werewolf horror films made?

Howl-lywood, California.

How do you greet Dracula after not seeing him for a while?

"Welcome, bat."

Can Dracula be trusted?

He has a count ability.

What is a scary creature's favorite time of day?

Moaning time.

What kind of pants d ghosts wear?

Boo jeans.

If adult ghosts wear sheets, what do baby ghosts wear?

Pillowcases.

What kind of bees come out at night in the graveyard?

Zom-bees.

Which scary creature checked himself into the mental hospital?

Frankenstein's monster: he realized he had a screw loose.

Why do zombies take naps?

They are dead-tired.

How does the zombie with rotting flesh smell?

Through his nose.

What do ghosts have up their noses?

Boo-gers.

What do ghosts do when winter ends?
Spring screaming.

Where did Hatchet Man buy his hatchet?
At the chopping mall.

What scary creature models clothes?
A wear wolf.

What is the toughest scary creature to please at the Spooksville Comedy Club?

The ghost: all he wants to do is boo.

What happened when the demonized football player nearly fumbled the ball?

He retained possession.

How do demons describe their delightful Halloween?

"We had a devil of a time!"

What kind of mistake do spooks make?

Boo-boos.

What is it called when a ghost scares the wrong person?

A boo boo-boo.

Why don't ghosts wear deodorant?

They like to keep it super-natural.

What kind of demons drive their cars super fast?

Speed demons.

How do ghosts take their coffee?

With one scream and two sugars.

What branch of the U.S. Service did the zombie join?

The Marine Corpse.

What is the object of zombie football?

To get the ball over the ghoul line.

What did the baby tree say on Halloween night when it went door-to-door collecting candy?

"Twig or treat."

What did the baby clock say on Halloween night when it opened its candy bag for someone to fill it?

"Tick or treat."

What kind of snakes do noisy skeletons keep as pets?

Rattlersnakes.

What do bats like to do in their free time?

Hang around together.

A ghost-hunter in a haunted house was followed by a pair of mysterious curtains. What happened when the ghosthunter ran out of the house?

He was saved from curtain death.

What games do scary creatures like to play in the graveyard?

Name that Tomb and Truth or Scare.

What scary creature is good at keeping secrets?

The mummy knows how to keep things under wraps.

What scary creature is self-absorbed?

Mummies are all wrapped up in themselves.

Why was the skeleton never going to be a hero?

No guts; no glory.

Why do skeletons hate winter?

They get chilled to the bone and the cold goes right through them.

What kind of lines do ghosts like to fly in; is it in vertical lines?

No; they prefer horror-zontal lines.

What did the little spirit who enjoyed writing want to be when he grew up?

A ghost writer.

What did Dracula say when he came to the end of the chapter in the jokebook?

"Fangs for the laughs."

How do you make garlic toast?

Raise your glass and compliment it.

What kind of rocks do scary creatures like to collect?

Tomb stones.

What board game do scary creatures like to play?

Moan-opoly.

Why is the grave digger never bored?

There is always plots to do.

Which scary creature cusses a lot?

The swear wolf.

What sound does a crying ghost make?

Boo-o-o-o-o-o-o-o-hoo.

How evil are skeletons?

They are bad to the bone.

What kind of scary creatures sell cookies?

Ghoul Scouts.

What kind of party do scary creatures throw?

A monster party.

FUN FACTS FOR HALLOWEEN

Do you know which US state produces the most pumpkins?

Illinois produces five times more pumpkins than other states, it has 15,000 acres of land for growing pumpkins, and grows over 500 million pounds of them per year!

Do you know what the fastest speed is for someone carving a pumpkin?

Stephen Clarke from New York managed to carve a pumpkin with eyes, nose, mouth and ears, in just 16.47 seconds, in 2013!

CHAPTER BOO
Puns

"Where there is no imagination, there is no horror."
~ **Arthur Conan Doyle**

When someone comes up behind me and shouts, "Boo!," I am so startled that I usually jump and even let out a little squeak.

The following Halloween jokes are puns, which are sentences/words that can say two things at once. In many cases, the first meaning is easy to grasp, but the second will sneak up and surprise you; many people don't even see the second meaning unless someone points it out to them. See how many of the double-meanings you can find.

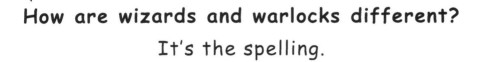

How are wizards and warlocks different?

It's the spelling.

How did the girl find the wizard?

Charming.

What two keys are needed to unlock a haunted house?

A skeleton key and a spook key.

How mature does a ghost joke need to be before it is shared?

Full groan.

What kind of books do ghosts like to read?

Ones with a good plot - a cemetery plot.

Why do disgruntled ghosts stay in the basement of the haunted house?

It's the whine cellar.

Why did the ghost have to go to the hospital?

To have his ghoul stones removed.

Where do scary things go to listen to live concerts?

The rave-yard.

How should you apologize if you accidently share a Halloween joke before Halloween season?

"I spook too soon."

When the ghost disappeared into the fog, were people lonely for him?

He certainly was mist.

What are you experiencing if you find yourself in a creepy place and think you've been there before?

Deja boo.

Why did the haunted house let out a scream?

It had windowpane.

Who pays for the upkeep of the haunte house?

It's a fun dead (funded) project.

Why was the overweight ghost working out at the gym?

He was trying to get down to a medium.

Do corpses get tired?

They are dead on their feet.

What happened when the big bucket saw a ghost?

It became a little pale.

What do flesh-eating monsters eat in their salad?

Human romaines.

What happens when two mad scientists get together?

You get a paradox (pair of docs).

What did the bodiless left hand say to the bodiless right hand?

How does it feel to always be right?

How did the witch fortune teller want her steak cooked?

Medium.

Do witches use cellphones to tell time?

No. They prefer to use their witch watch.

What did Momma Monster yell at Daddy Monster when he started to daydream?

"Are you even listening to me? It looks like what I say goes in one ear and out the other seven?"

Why did the creepy spider sign a contract with the New York Yankees?

The spider was great at catching flies.

What kind of flooring does the Day-Scare Child Center have?

Infant-tile.

What did the ghost-hunter say when he noticed the curtains were drawn?

"I hope nothing else in this house is just a sketch."

What do you call it when a ghost-hunter goes to the gym?

Exercising.

What did the adult monster say to the teenage monster at the family reunion?

"You gruesome."

49

Does the Invisible Man have any kids?

No. He's not a parent (apparent).

What do you call a corpse that is pushing on your doorbell?

A dead ringer.

What did the ticklish pumpkin say to the carver?

"That tickles; cut it out!"

What did the warlock say when the witch secretly switched his butter for her butter substitute made of newt?

"I can't believe it's newt butter!"

Does Dracula play poker?

No, he doesn't like anything to do with stakes.

How does the average monster burger taste?

Meaty ogre.

Why did the zombie hope the jury would arrive at a guilty verdict as his trial?

He wanted the judge to give him life.

Which scary creature is the rudest at the dinner table?

Gobblin.

How did the monster who claimed to be a vegetarian justify eating a factory, people and all?

He said it was a plant.

What corpse works at city hall?

The night mayor (nightmare).

Why are demons fat

They hate exorcising

How do we know the warlock is feeling better?

He was up for a spell today.

What compliment did the corpse get at the Halloween party?

People kept telling her that she looked life-like.

Why did the witch retire from fortune telling?

She no longer saw a future.

Why did the woman insist on carrying a first-aid kit with bandages everywhere she went?

She had mummy issues.

Why is Dracula so pessimistic?

He drank some B Negative.

Who do jack o' lanterns have great respect for?

Scarecrows; they have been looking up to scarecrows since they were little pumpkin seedlings.

Why did the witch load her broom's saddlebags with baseballs?

She heard there would be bats flying in the sky

What scary creature owns a store?

A ware wolf.

What do zombies mean when they say their mind is made up?

They mean it is imaginary.

What do you say to the Headless Horseman when he drops his head?

"Dude, get a hold of yourself."

Where is cell phone service not available at the cemetery?

It is a dead zone.

What invitation does Dracula offer his dinner guests?

"Can I interest you in a bite?"

When does the Headless Horseman allow his horse to talk?

Whinny wants to.

What flying dinosaur was the scariest of all dinosaurs?

The terror-dactyl

What does the mummy like to do at the end of the day?

Unwind.

What do you call the letters from admirers which Dracula receives?

Fang mail.

Why should you cover your ears around a witch?

She uses a lot of cursive language.

What happened when Dracula fell asleep at the New Year's Eve party?

There was a countdown.

How do you refer to women who are fans and admirers of Dracula?

Bat crazy.

What happened when Dracula sold stolen merchandise on an Internet site?

A count suspended.

Why did Dracula avoid the meat aisle at the grocery store?

He didn't want to risk a steak to his heart.

Why did the scarecrow refuse the Halloween candy?

He was stuffed.

Why did the alcoholi ghost-hunter hunt ghosts?

For the boos.

Why did the busy skeleton not fix his shattered rib cage?

His heart wasn't in it.

What is the name of the Italian restauran where corpses serve spook-ghetti and ghoul-ash?

Pasta Way.

After the warlock turned the bear into a princess, how did the princess behave?

She was unbearable.

Why do vampires prefer human blood over turkey blood?

Turkey blood is fowl.

What scary creature is a philosopher?

Aware wolf.

Which scary creature discusses its illnesses?

The vampire constantly talks about his coughin'.

What kind of pictures do scary creatures paint?

Monsterpieces.

What is Dracula being when he stands in front of you saying, "Hi, beautiful," takes a step backwards and says, "Hi, beautiful," and takes yet another step backward and says, "Hi, beautiful"?

A pain in the neck.

Who is the smartest scary creature?

Frank Enstein.

Why did Dracula decide not to be an investment banker?

He didn't like stakeholders.

Why did Dracula go to the baseball stadium?

He was told the players were looking for a new bat.

Is it easy to get rid of any vampires in your home?

It is light work.

Which scary creature is the greatest weightlifter?

The mad scientist Dr. Frankenstein; he is quite a body builder.

Why did the witch who loved sports take her broom to the baseball stadium?

She heard the home team was going to try to sweep.

How is this chapter like a re-taped mummy?

It's wrapped up.

Which scary creature seeks to further his life?

The Headless Horseman wants to get ahead.

How is a good joke teller like Dr. Frankenstein?

Both will leave you in stitches.

FUN FACTS FOR HALLOWEEN

How often do you think there's a full moon on Halloween?

It only actually occurs 3-4 times in 100 years!

Do you know what the Halloween festival is called in China?

Teng Chieh or the Lantern Festival. At the festival lanterns shaped like dragons and other animals are put around the streets, intended to guide spirits to earthly homes.

CHAPTER THRILL
Silly Scenarios

"On Halloween you get to become anything that you want to be." ~ **Ava Dellaira**

Halloween is full of thrills – the thrill of getting candy, the thrill that comes from getting scared when you see scary masks, and the thrill that comes from sharing good jokes with good friends. The following are short, silly scenes. Each can be read within just a couple of minutes. Enjoy!

A seven-foot tall seven-footed monster walked up to a gas station pump, took the hose from the pump, and put the hose in his mouth. The attendant saw him and yelled from the safety of the store, "You have got to have a car to use that." The monster replied, **"I had one for lunch. Now I'm trying to wash it down."**

Having just stolen all the Halloween candy from the warehouse where it was being stored for an upcoming Halloween Festival, a witch and a wizard were driving in their car trying to get away from the police. As the police closed in, he wizard suggested, **"Can you turn this car to an alley?"**

People of the past did not have a good grasp of science, and therefore they attributed a lot of things they could not understand to fairies and superstition. In the Middle Ages, people believed that the undead – people who were dead but who had come back to earth returned every October 31, when a wrinkle in time allowed them to transition from their world to ours. People often set food out for them, believing if the undead ate they would continue their journey to get back to their body in the graveyard and then to the world of the undead. Some tricksters realized if they wore masks, they could not be told apart from the undead, and therefore the undead would not bother them. These tricksters then went door-to-door, collecting food. (We still wear masks and go door-to-door collecting food on Halloween evening today.) The tricksters also did things they should not have done, such as knocking over tombstones or destroying property. **The tricksters, of course, blamed the undead if anyone asked them about it.**

The fad of witches riding brooms is sweeping th
nation. I wonder, if people get car-sick riding
the car, **do witches get broom-sick riding c
their brooms?**

Clickety-clack. Clickety-clack. The freight trai
lumbered down the creaking rails. High-spee
trains used to go through here decades ago, bu
today the rails could only handle slow, slow train:
Whereas twenty trains used to pass daily, toda

ily one switcher makes a weekly run. The icety-clack sounds and the constant vibrations oke up the ghost of the hobo from his slumber the corner of the boxcar. He rubbed the sleep om his eyes and curiously focused his gaze on ie day's cargo - female sheep. There were emale sheep everywhere; he realized he must ive gone to sleep trying to count them. Noticing ie ghost was awake, one of the sheep raised its ead to let out a warning to the others. "Don't be ared," the ghost pleaded, held his arm out in a riendly gesture, and began taking a step toward ie wooly creature. The sheep replied, **"Stop ght there. Don't come any closer. We're a reight of ewe."**

A boy and a girl were walking hand-in-hand up hillside when they happened to notice that th moon was full. The boy slowly started to grow fu as the girl watched in surprise as well as horror. "My gosh!" she claimed, "You're a wolf The boy replied calmly, **"Yes, I'm aware."**

It's human nature to deny responsibility whe we do something wrong; we are also prone to tr to blame somebody else rather than accep responsibility Since the **Halloween prank** **happened in autumn, guess who got the blam** **for the mischief - the Fall Guy.**

ittle Lisa was in school the day after Halloween. er teacher wanted to test her math skills, so e asked, "If you have ten pieces of candy from ick-or-treating and someone asks you for two, w many pieces of candy will you have?" Lisa plied, "Ten. I refuse to share." The teacher phrased the question, "Instead of asking for e candy, let's say that your friend takes two eces of candy from you. Now what will you ave?" Lisa replied, **"Ten pieces of candy and a rmer friend."**

After turning on the television horror movi the teenage girl cuddled next to her boyfrier with her bowl of fruit. "Fruit and a horr movie?" he asked. She replied, **"I like to e peaches and scream."**

FUN FACTS FOR HALLOWEEN

How long does it take you to hollow out and carve a pumpkin?

It takes me ages, and even longer to clean up the mess!

Do you know that in Alabama certain Halloween costumes are banned?

It is against the law to dress up as a priest or nun on Halloween! You can be fined or arrested if you do.

CHAPTER GORE
Knock-Knock

"Sticky fingers, tired feet; one last house,
trick or treat!" ~ **Rusty Fischer**

Haunted houses are full of gore, scary
sounds, and weird knocks, so it is fitting
Chapter Gore looks at who is knocking at the
door. I don't think it will be a skeleton; they
get chilled to the bone too fast to be outside
in this autumn weather. Let's see who it is:

KNOCK, KNOCK.

Who's there?

Gino.

Gino who?

**Gino who or what you are going to
dress up as for Halloween?**

KNOCK, KNOCK.

Who's there?

Ghost.

Ghost who?

Ghost stand by the front door; I'll be ready in a minute.

KNOCK, KNOCK.
Who's there?
A Band.
A Band who?
Abandon all hope, all who go to the haunted house.

KNOCK, KNOCK.
Who's there?
Voodoo.
Voodoo who?
Voodoo you think you're fooling in that Halloween costume?

KNOCK, KNOCK.
Who's there?
Weirdo.
Weirdo who?
Weirdo you want to go trick-or-treating this year?

KNOCK, KNOCK.

Who's there?

Bat.

Bat who?

Bat you didn't expect to hear knock-knock jokes today.

KNOCK, KNOCK.
Who's there?
Armageddon.
Armageddon who?
Armageddon out of here if this pla
is haunted!

KNOCK, KNOCK.
Who's there?
Mikey.
Mikey who?
Mikey won't open the door to your
room or the haunted house.

KNOCK, KNOCK.
Who's there?
Gargoyle.
Gargoyle who?
Gargoyle with mouthwash; you have
bat breath. Your breath smells
worse than garlic.

KNOCK, KNOCK.

Who's there?

Tomb.

Tomb who?

Tomb it may concern, please ignore our silly laughter; we are telling knock-knock jokes.

KNOCK, KNOCK.
Who's there?
Miss Tickle.
Miss Tickle who?
Miss Tickle (mystical) things are sa
to happen on Halloween.

KNOCK, KNOCK.
Who's there?
Alfred O.
Alfred O who?
Alfred O ghosts; are you afraid too

KNOCK, KNOCK.
Who's there?
A Tick.
A Tick who?
A Tick is where most ghosts prefer
to hide; very few choose the
basement.

KNOCK, KNOCK.

Who's there?

Scaredy Cat.

Scaredy Cat who?

Scaredy cat and then scare the dog.

KNOCK, KNOCK.
Who's there?
Gore Juice.
Gore Juice who?
Gore Juice costumes are on display
some of the best I have ever seen.

KNOCK, KNOCK.
Who's there?
Wendy.
Wendy who?
Wendy sun sets, trick-or-treaters
come out.

KNOCK, KNOCK.
Who's there?
Miss Stout.
Miss Stout who?
Miss Stout on some good Halloween
jokes, but I've got more.

KNOCK, KNOCK.

Who's there?

Spider.

Spider who?

Spider looking at us; spied him looking at us too.

KNOCK, KNOCK.
Who's there?
Toad.
Toad who?
Toad-ally ready for Halloween.

KNOCK, KNOCK.
Who's there?
Philip.
Philip who?
Philip my candy bag please.

KNOCK, KNOCK.
Who's there?
Fry Ten.
Fry Ten who?
Fry Ten all of the ghosts so they don't frighten us.

KNOCK, KNOCK.

Who's there?

Candies.

Candies who?

Candies knock-knock jokes keep going for another hour?

KNOCK, KNOCK.

Who's there?

Grave.

Grave who?

Grave-y is great with mashed potatoes.

KNOCK, KNOCK.

Who's there?

Zombies.

Zombies who?

Zombies were buzzing inside the flower I was going to pick for mom, so I didn't pick it after all.

KNOCK, KNOCK.

Who's there?

Disguise.

Disguise who?

Disguise pretty serious about knock-knock jokes.

FUN FACTS FOR HALLOWEEN

Do you know it's not only people who dress up on Halloween?

Dogs are commonly dressed up at Halloween, as pumpkins, hot dogs, lions, pirates, bumblebees, devils, superheroes and other amusing outfits.

Do you know why people didn't Trick or Treat during WWII?

It's because sugar was rationed and there wasn't enough to make sweets.

Did you enjoy the book?

If you did, we are ecstatic. If not, please write your complaint to us and we will ensure we fix it.

If you're feeling generous, there is something important that you can help me with – tell other people that you enjoyed the book.

Ask a grown-up to write about it on Amazon. When they do, more people will find out about the book. It also lets Amazon know that we are making kids around the world laugh. Even a few words and ratings would go a long way.

If you have any ideas or jokes that you think are super funny, please let us know. We would love to hear from you. Our email address is - **riddleland@riddlelandforkids.com**

Riddleland Bonus Book

http://pixelfy.me/riddlelandbonus

Thank you for buying this book. We would like to share a special bonus as a token of appreciation. It is a collection of 50 original jokes, riddles, and two super funny stories!

Join our **Facebook Group**
at **Riddleland for Kids** to get
daily jokes and riddles.

Would you like your jokes and riddles to be featured in our next book?

We are having a contest to see who are the smartest or funniest boys and girls in the world! :

1) **Creative and Challenging Riddles**
2) **Tickle Your Funny Bone Contest**

Parents, please email us your child's "Original" Riddle or Joke and **he or she could win a $50 Amazon gift card and be featured in our next book.**

Here are the rules:

1) It must be challenging for the riddles and funny for the jokes!
2) It must be 100% original and not something from the Internet! It is easy to find out!
3) You can submit both jokes and riddles as they are 2 separate contests.
4) No help from the parents unless they are as funny as you.
5) Winners will be announced via email or our Facebook group – Riddleland for kids
6) Please also mention what book you purchased.
7) Email us at Riddleland@riddlelandforkids.com

Other Fun Children Books for Kids!

Riddles Series

It's Laugh O'Clock Joke Books

It's Laugh O'Clock-Would You Rather?

About Riddleland

As parents, the biggest riddle we face is always, "Am I doing this parenting thing right?" Well, Riddleland is here to answer that question for you, and the answer is a resounding, "We have no idea because we're parents, too."

Riddleland believes that families are the most important thing in this world, and everything we do is for them. That's why we take extra care when creating innovative, fun, and age-appropriate concepts that help your kids think critically, enjoy reading, and simply be their wonderful selves. That's why we go above and beyond to support families by having a tremendous supply of actually-useful resources for kids, parents, and educators. And — most importantly — that's why we donate to support children and families in the U.S. and abroad, who don't have much access to fun and educational books, and why we hire fellow, working-parents to help create our hilarious jokes, hand-drawn illustrations, mindblowing trivia, and absurd would-you-rather questions that we double-dog dare you to read without laughing.

Pack up the kids (okay, not literally) and take a mental vacation to Riddleland to laugh, learn, and live in the moment.

If you have suggestions for us or want to work with us, shoot us an email at **riddleland@riddlelandforkids.com**

Our family's favorite quote:

"Creativity is an area in which younger people have a tremendous advantage since they have an endearing habit of always questioning past wisdom and authority."
~ Bill Hewlett

Made in the USA
Middletown, DE
12 October 2022

12614087R00053